Cool Head

Eva Lewarne

ISBN: 978-93-90601-22-6

First Edition: 2022
Rs. 200/-

Cyberwit.net
HIG 45 Kaushambi Kunj, Kalindipuram
Allahabad - 211011 (U.P.) India
http://www.cyberwit.net
Tel: +(91) 9415091004
E-mail: info@cyberwit.net

Contents

a god particle

scientist are now ahead
of religions gone dead
trying to claim god for themselves
others gone to hell
including scientists
who believe eternity
can be dissected and manipulated
particles of god dissipated
to empower the corpoate elite
to fatten their balance sheet
to fatten their bellies and greed
no accountability for their deed
scientists are beholding to them
for money and support
no accountability for what they score
and who does what with their find
did they find a particle of
god's behind?

a bird got my wings

a bird got my wings
I lost them and a few other things
when a gale blew me over,
flat on my face, what a disgrace

the bird preened awhile,
then donned my wings
and flew away with no regrets

my soul, stranded
roamed the earth flightless
while ice lay threats
making me lifeless

awaiting spring, for the return
of a bird with my wings
to soar once more
beyond the rain of sorrow

I turn my face to the sun
the soft warm breeze
of tomorrow and tomorrow

As She Stomps

as she stomped the earth, heels sunken in green grass
caressing with each step the long blades
she longed for rebirth into a new place, new city, new life
saturated with poetry and emotions and color
not the cold, steel, concrete jungle aspiring
towards the sky like the CN Tower

as she stomped the grass its new shoots crying for birth
unnoticed by her feet plowing forward fretfully
pointing homeward, anxiously, where he sat
immobile in their plush chair waiting for dinner impatiently

as she stomped home she realized that while frolicking in the park
communing with trees, she had forgotten his needs

as her eyes rounded with fear seeing where he sat
resting his curled fist on the armchair ready to spring
and beat her up without notice or query about anything
her feet heavy and her face weary awaiting the sting
of blows that will make her eyes smart and her ears ring

as she lies in a heap on the floor she wonders if there is more
than this life, this city, this place and whether she has the courage to go
she closes her eyes with a sigh as the door clicks after he is gone
and she sees angels circling above urging her on

a tool

this tool is a pink, rough, thick and ugly
prone to creating either peace or war
a truth sayer, a liar, a moaner, a crier
a cajoler, a bullshitter and more
by clicking and clacking it gives dispensations
on how to view the world
and you had better stay tall and mum
about it all to fit in
or else you will be ousted from the inner circle
of the bores that knit pick with their tongues
shredding your soul

this tool can also soothe, sigh, sympathize
and comfort away hurts in your life
by telling the truth and even white lies
and above all it tastes good when eating fudge
or kissing in a french way

this tool can be pure pleasure
if you are rolling in the hay
this tool is the mighty tongue
belonging to all and every one
ugly as it is when ripped out of its juicy lips
without it we would be silent which is no fun

cool head

she greeted each sinner with, a .."hi, it's lovely not to be cold"
In the temple of spirits as she glided by looking each one in the eye
as if to say "take warmth in the service today because the end is nigh"
cold cancer held her in it's grip, hours of retching and a shamelessly
nude head led her to say, "it's lovely not to be cold today"
grateful to be alive, she preaches from the pulpit, .."to count your
blessings
when upon life's bellows you are tossed…", no matter how tempting
heaven
may appear at the right hand of god

van gogh's sunflowers sit below the pulpit flickering yellow
by candle-light reminding of sunny days and wide-toothed smiles
as if to say, "no matter what sins you have committed, you will be
acquitted", hope for a mere pence on sunday knowing on monday you
will dance in hell again but for now, immersed in sandalwood and
myrrh she forgets
the smell of sulphur from the cocktail of her cancer-curing brew

standing tall under mary, mother of god, a halo of hair soft as downy
growing back in proudly she smiles at the congregation beguiled
in rapt stillness sensing death has been outwitted and god appeased
somehow at least for now while she preaches of love and forgiveness
and how lovely it is to be cool headed once more when warm
blood flows
thru your veins making you join the living instead of a dead corpse
floating on the shore of human dross hoping for entry into heaven

cancer not loss gave her the entrance ticket to ecstasy instead
here on earth and she wants to share it with all the burdened souls
in the pews listening intently to her words of wisdom, warmth,
comfort and coolness as she speaks of hope because she knows
that nothing else comes close to finding the word that will ease
their load and help them appreciate how lovely it is not be cold

Fool

green man, woman of Spring wielding sword in air
thru empty space of rainbow heart
unlocking horns of Bacchus, unconscious
of the tiger tearing at his side
forever stopping to smell fresh new shoots
on budding branches of ancient, wise oaks
bulging eyes piercing thru heavy stale air
tossing his fool's cap, splitting his sides with
resounding laughter he takes up the dare
to dance like a child in celebration of life
biding his time waiting to die, folly be hanged!
grey man, woman of Mind abstracting reality sublime
your hundredth tom of verse gathering dust, laden with words
mechanically marching single file across blank, bleak pages of
sterile residuals from processed green trees, now dead door stops
buried beneath stacks of library atrocities
in bacchanalian ecstasy, consumed by fire, water simultaneously
the disc of earth uncovers buried treasure of freedom
folly, fun, purity of a child's fantasy
the fool will spin magic in tall grasses of morning sun
or the rich shadows of a waning moon
like a rainbow after the rain, he tames the tiger of our brain

A Game of Non-Chess

Sitting across the square table was a tall angular man, a Magi
"Are we playing chess I asked?" He grinningly said, "non-chess,
this is a game without rules, like a poem without words
like reading a blank page and seeing the next move,
understood?"

A test? I panic!
"Once the game starts, there is no turning back, it's life or death",
then pounding the flimsy table with his fists he adds,
"Your journey has been long, it's time you knew what to do,
thinking will not save you.

My mind becomes blank like the white page of a blank book
"That's better", he says, patting me on the back making my
shoulders inflamed, until only cinders remain,
a gift of non-chess to be played until I win or die trying
The Magi vanishes, leaving me gently crying

Tears of joy...

Here I Am

Here I am like every noon, my morning
sitting in my well worn chair in front of my well used screen
with my turkish coffee mug to the right, a dear friend
praying it doesn't singe my keyboard again
The screen, my friend that never talks back
that laughs with me, not at me, trusty when working
a path to a life I really don't have
but hopeful someday I may

Here I am again waiting for the end of rain
for the skies to open to let me play in sunshine
in happiness in peace, in bliss

Away from the screen that burns my lids with tears
telling stories of woes, killings and fears
death, death, death, death, death and yet
I turn it on every noon hopeful once again
that it will deliver me from boredom and pain
let me know my life as is, the life of a common man
has not been lived in vain.
hey it is all okay

can't get up, can't lie down
face screwed up into a frown
another sleepless night, pointless day
but hey, all's okay, so they say
fat cells turned to stem
will pave the way

we will all be young again
never die, maybe visit Spain
forever living, forever frowning
forever drowning in debt
to those that call the shots
mostly bots

bots as cashiers, as sex toys
as CEOs, as playboys
as mothers, as pets
as vets

not plastic, made from hemp
revived again, by rain
alive forever to shop
what can't be bought
love and all that rot

when nothing is left but bots
with fake smiles
sucking fat cells from corpses
not saved by facebook styles
or bot horses

but hey, it is all okay

hope

hope, a poor man's hammer of staving off depression
of unfulfilled dreams and wishes
no hope, no fear, someone said
but what happens when hope is gone
giving birth to ever-ending desire
a desire that burns bright
eating out the insides of your gut

hope, a poor man's tool to stave off hunger for more
a hopeless turmoil of the soul
let the hammer drop on hope, face your fears
give in to your tears of desire
and maybe your burning fire will subside
into a peaceful acceptance of your lot
a tranquility of just being, with no hope

just dance

whenever a feather oh so bright alights on your brain at night
tickling your fancy, trembling your mind, like a leaf on a vine
kissed by an abyss of dark rich mist
enhancing the whiteness of its cist
cradling bodies in throes of mourn, knowing that
all well placed plans in this life have to end
and in the morn a new body will be born

whenever you are left with remorse, forgetting the force
the light source the joyous bliss of heaven's kiss
a feather will arrive to open your eyes and ears to hear
the steady hum of silence, of life itself
don't fear the darkness, the pain, and the bad weather
for magic permeates that feather

whenever you've been tickled by a white feather
it will shake loose your very cells of bad spells
old cob webs of disappointed disenchantment
renewing your faith in the cosmic clown or cosmic chance
that released you into this space to dance
labamba and more…in a trance…
just dance and dance

Just Sleep

you want to sleep and nothing else
you want to end the monotony of
eternally motionless days punctuated
by snacks and nothing else
“here is your cocoa Tony”, she croons
you answer, ‘thanks” after a long pause
and hold the drink in your trembling hands
with effort you lift the glass to your lips
and carefully swallow a few sips
then two, then finish it to the end
only to await dinner and nothing else

after eating you want to sleep and nothing else
you are lifted like a child from your chair
and placed in a bed, with your diaper changed
the whole process void of romance
you want to sleep but sleep eludes you
instead you find yourself in a dark cool forest
where wild animals play, fight and fornicate
a wolf grabs your leg between sharp teeth
without piercing your skin, and you feel no pain
although your heart skips a beat and you try
to call out in vain

a stranger appears and says, “feel grateful
that you are walking and young and well”
and you wonder whether you have landed in hell
a blue cool breeze caresses your face and no flames
surround, quite the opposite, peace and beauty abound

in the morn you awaken only to find the same
motionless body in bed with diaper wet
the forest was so real you are now confused, irate
and can not bear to remain one more day in that state

you retreat into the cave of your mind like a wounded animal
the wounds salty from all the unshed tears
from years of hard labour and loveless wives' vicious tongues
jagged edges of pain made round and smooth, worn
by accumulated dampness of a million hurts
you would rather run with the wolves than be
an over pampered lapdog here on earth
rather than a long life you just want eternal
sleep and nothing else

last raven

the ebon raven was first and will be last
empowered with grace he made of
the matte midnight black, his quest
rich blackness cool to the eyes
magic mystery giving rise
to an intense infinite moonlit surprise
like the elusive quality of Van Gogh's *starry night*
a timeless boundless sight
beckoning us to be still like the raven
patiently awaiting the end of night
his feathers sleek and shining bright
neither here nor there between two worlds
trying to decide which path to fly, left or right

trusting the moon to be friendly he stands his ground
engulfed by vast black space awaiting a sign
omen or sound knowing the one taste of grace
until then here he will stay facing the moon
beyond his reach until the light of day
will shine on the face he wore even before
the one he had prior to the world being born
fixed to the spot he holds fast, marooned
as live currents run along his head and breast
this raven is happy to just be, at last
a part of the universe, in ebon harmony
according to ancient myth he brought light to the world
and will take it back when he leaves
the ebon raven was first and will be last

I Love You

I love you because you flit and flicker in my life
creating shadow worlds gone by
an illusion of the *north wind* blowing hard
to wipe away cobwebs of a hard life
viewed with fresh eyes

I love you because you have no beginning, no end
round and round you go, and never bend
under the weight of cooling my room, cooling my head

I love you, dear fan, especially today
in scorching heat of forty-five degrees
as I sit comfortably on my settee, feet up
watching you flit, creating a breeze

Spinning stories of devas
dancing bare-foot and free, beckoning
to play away from the heat
in a parallel universe not yet seen
yet inferred, fleetingly caught in mind's eye
of flit and flicker, of times gone by

I love you today and tomorrow too
for when the frost arrives outside I put you on
to bring the heat down from the roof

And you do keep me toasty and warm
and dancing to the never-ending song
of life today and tomorrow and more

flitting and flickering and spinning lore
so round and round I go singing your song.

moans and creaks

the workout bike moaned
when i traveled in place
in the early morn

then my shoes moaned
when i walked home
from the gym

moans rang on the upstairs climb
even the door groaned when ajar
it was a moaning sort of time

dead mushy leaves on the ground
grey skies, early night, no dusk
only a moaning sound

soft rains dewed the earth
while chilly winds bent trees
creaking in the breeze

my body moans and creaks
at every turn
even in my sleep

only my mind laughs
at this pitiful moaning affair
of birthing, of aging, of dying
of heaven and hell

One Little Virus

humans' great intellect has reached it's peak
in the pursuit of mindless comforts for the rich
and explorations of useless space odysseys
an apostasy of abandoned hope for an eden
on earth where all were happy and free

stepping over the homeless in the street
reminded us that was not be

some hoarded the key with their insatiable greed
and heartless indifference that loosed to rule man's fate
the heart relegated to an icon on the mechanical screen
so the rich could eat their money for breakfast

all it took was scaring the rich with death and disease
for them to become suddenly meek
and find homes for the weary sleeping in the streets
and food for the masses feasting from rubbish bins

one little virus unleashed and money goes poof, up in smoke
and the intellect realizes that it was never in charge at all
back end tester group

the back end tester group emailed me today
selling instant penis growth for free
just by popping a pill I can give my girlfriend a thrill
by growing my pinkie times three

what it might do to me they didn't say
would I need to keep it folded and hidden away
maybe my tailor might need to re-size my pants
so my attribute wouldn't be too obvious at first glance
to the ladies who might be tempted to trail after me
and not allow me to be

who are the back end testers anyway
are they different from the front end testers
do they lead with their front end or behind
all these questions were foremost on my mind
when I opened my hotmail today
and by the way did I say that I was born
minus a pinkie and am not gay

the scammers should first do their research
before my email they search
maybe in my next life I might need the advice
of the back end tester group
but not today, as a front end tester woman I will stay

poor but elegant

poor but elegant was her motto
a life well lived though never traveled
farther than the corner store
is that all there is she thought, no more?

poor of material possessions
she sat cross-legged with nothing to lose
ignorant of any recessions
looking inward as her toes hit the roof
racing up to her brain and then
back again until she went poof

poor and invisible, to others and herself
the others were afraid to look beyond her poverty
and she, she knew that ultimately she wasn't really there
what was there to dress and who was there to care?

poor of vitals and glands but elegant
in the placement of her hands
she sat awaiting her destiny to be free
of responsibility, awaiting to become the sea

elegantly she peered into nothingness
discovering beauty in her vivid dreams
and what she created on canvas with paint
challenging herself to see more than the eye can behold
actually blessed to be alive if all is to be told

poor but elegant suited her lifestyle
of stillness and space inside and out
a hollow tube of air, lit and unlit
unimpeded by the outside world

Putting it Down

The sound of one hand clapping can be a slap in the face
She lived encumbered with religious icons and clichés
their iconic voices screaming loudly to obey
buddha heads marching single file
plastered on large canvasses to beguile
the unwary artist, who doesn't trust her own icons
torn from a source unknown….the unborn.

and hung by the hem of their demands,
blind to who she is…who she is…
spinning useless words in her brain
all coiled into a spring of lies
waiting for a final demise.

Art helped to ease the pain of her deadened heart
each thread unraveled one at a time, she learned to put it down
inching on like a blind caterpillar straining to hear her song
to see the light at the end of the tunnel, she forged on
before religion it was her mother who knew her better
then she knew herself and made her eternally grateful
for being a worm on a hook of no consequence or matter

the all-knowing fish-mother told her what to think and what to wear
until she didn't dare to have a voice of her own
for fear of unbridled wrath spewing from her fishy groin
later on religion become the omnipotent womb
sealing her lips into a closed tomb

Stubbornly for years she hung on not believing
she had a right to exist until one bright morn
she saw the error of her ways and got mighty pissed
she dreamt that finally the AGO gave her a small show
and lo and behold some art students marched in holding
large canvasses of buddha heads and hung them
obliterating her small feeble artistic attempts

she threw them out, saying that although her voice maybe small
it is hers and fine, maybe even divine from before she was born,
she remembered what a Zen Master once said,
"If you see a Buddha on the road, kill him."
Which she did, and the students fled and she put it down.

Raven Café

too poor to travel, too many responsibilities
she sat in a café sipping lattes, a poor man's treat
there she read about others who traveled afar
were free and flew to the farthest stars

one day a shiny blue-black raven came
knocking on the window and whispered her name…
cra cra cra…silently he said
your darkest fears must be shed

soar with me to regions yet unknown, be bold
alight on my ebon wings, take hold of my strength, be born
and cra cra cra to your heart's content
in the gold glittering early morn

the ebon of the void beckoned me
while I was fitted for a raven's mask and dress
blue-black tresses fluttering in the breeze
facilitating my magical flight with ease

instantly transported to another café
one full of oracles and powerful omens
the raven, a protector of prophets and poets
sat peacefully awaiting me, sipping a Moets

he said, "go sit on a wire be like me, foot-loose and fancy free
fly swiftly towards your destiny…"
listening with my heart I knew my latte days had lapsed
opening a chapter on a story fitted with many magical maps

as I wait for more chapters to unfold…
cra cra cra cra cra cra cra cra cra
cra cra cra cra cra cra cra cra cra
cra cra cra cra cra cra cra cra cra

a rooster's revenge

a rooster crowed at half past eight
but sunrise peaked long ago
leaving the people sleeping late
their chores undone, their beds unmade
where have the children gone

the cocky cock, an early riser
had never missed greeting the sun in the morn
perhaps a mishap, perhaps a wrong turn
had made him sleep in so long

indeed where have the children gone
dead silence rings about the people's ears
no giggling, shrieks of delight or running feet
and people conjured up their worse fears
shouting for their children, and hit the street

Janie, Tommy, Gina, they could be heard
resounding in a cacophony of voices
some shrill, some booming, some even curse word
thrown in for lack of better choices

the rooster stopped crowing, his task completed
knowing his eminent importance had no rival
puffed up he sat watching the people defeated
no way would they laugh at him again
when yesterday in the mud and in the rain
they made him fight another cock
until they were both maimed

Sleeping with Fish

did you know that *sleeping with fish* is a mobsters' saying
when they dump offensive bodies into the ocean deep
where only fish for company their bones do keep
bones are laid to rest in the wet silence of ocean sands
no longer blackmailed by greedy hands

did you know i dream of sleeping with fish
where silence leaves me at peace
after dusk turns to night and the moonlight glows
fish turn into birds and birds swim below
I can be a bird or a fish depending on the day of the week

did you know we can have a garden in this concrete jungle
to ease the pain of honking traffic sirens
a place to see dusk creeping into trees and plants
whispering secrets yet untold but remembered
as the sun settles on rooftops unencumbered by anger
anger, the thrill that causes mobsters to kill
that blinds them to the beauty of the ocean deep
that stops them from taking the leap of seeing
what is above is also below, land or sea,
birds or fish, are all really them and me
i can swim or fly, just not at the same time

did you know that i can squawk like my feathered friends
but prefer the silence of ocean depths meditating with my gill-filled breath
above is fine but gliding and sleeping with fish below is best
letting my bones turn to philosophers stones in their resting place

at the bottom of the heap

she howled from hopelessness, from being at the bottom of the heap
a piercing shrill shriek of never-ending misery, abuse and indignity
forging for food you dumped in your dumpster in green-black plastic bags
the same ones the hopeless wrap themselves in, when it rains
where they sleep on cold cement in fear and hope of not being attacked
and maybe dying peacefully during the stupor of the night

but in the morn she again finds herself reborn to the life on the street
adorned with bags and rags and dreams of yesterday shattered once more
trying to embark on the wings of hope yet again to refrain from falling
in the dark deep pit of despair that makes her stand for hours in stillness
pretending to be a tree so no one will notice her and her indignity

she made a make-shift teepee in a square, a collection of odds
and ends, blankets, torn clothes and cardboard boxes and a red
bucket recently found that serves as a toilet to relieve herself, for
the cafes will not let her in unless she pays for that pleasure by
buying a bagel and mostly that is impossible because her pride
still doesn't allow her to beg
although some people with guilt written on their face will dump
some change by her side

as she howls in hopelessness, her stomach growls with hunger
and powerlessness
to satiate that need, as well as the other of companionship, being
loved and freed from the indignity of living in the street she
communes with the trees especially one maple that shelters her
from the worse rain and soothes her broken soul never to be
repaired again
the howl of hopelessness will awaken you from the deep sleep
you enjoy, dancing with sugar plums at night, in your comfy cozy
soft bed, covered with a quilt especially designed for you on your
birthday

and the howls will make you tremble and be sad and you will say
to yourself
hard luck, but for the grace of god you too could be sharing your
lot with the maple
belong to the have-nots instead of the haves and howl with
hopelessness when you can't bear it any more, her howls have
struck a cord and your tears drop to the floor
and for a moment you feel ennui, unable to focus, at a loss,
feeling hopeless
thinking that there is nothing worse than being at the bottom of
the heap living in the street, at least in death there is respite and
then you feel guilty for your thoughts and hope against hope that
someone will stop the governments from lining the pockets of the
rich so that they can not only eat but fly at will to Mars on a
whim, for don't they know that until she has a roof over her head
, the billionaire will never really be free and will howl in hopeless-
ness for all eternity and be allotted a spot at the bottom of the
heap in the life allotted to the dead

time

now einstein said, "…the reason for time
is so that everything doesn't happen at once…"
and he was great, so it must be true
coming from a great man of science
who couldn't possibly be wrong or lying
singing a song about time

now i say, "…the reason for time
is so the watchmakers can make dime…"
so the industrial wheel can let their clogs take lunch
and on a hunch i made time stand still, at will
by a little meditation, just by not moving mind
i realized that everything happens at once
and einstein was right

while sipping a latte at the sicilian one day
i watch the reaper arrive in may
in the guise of a man with a gun
shooting another sitting in the sun
a senseless act or divine intervention
i ask the great man, the big question
and what does einstein say?
"…time doesn't exist…" as he blows us a kiss
from the realm of timelessness

walking blues

when you walked out, the blues walked in
the house is empty and I am a'spin
down, down, towards the earth's core
wishing for time, wishing for more
wishing you were both still here

it's hugs that I miss the most
memories are a chilly ghost, without
laughter, warmth, heated debates
moonlit strolls, and soccer plays
salty tears over life's losses and wins

an old mother left behind, alone and tired
caught between heaven and hell
not quite ready to croak, put on a shelf
no longer the dynamo of her former self
removing her tooth before she eats

all the life's thrillers were but fillers
to while away the hours before the grim-reaper
knocks on my door and invites me to go
to my eternal home, as the rain beats
against the window pane of my soul

the house is empty inside and out
hope lingers on edges of my heart that
you will be happy, your lives bright
and I will survive, an old woman alone,
but not lonely reaching for what is holy

today my bones creak in wet weather
but tomorrow when the sun shines
maybe i might find buddha hidden
in the recesses of my mind
turning my walking blues to pink

this morning the sun refused to rise…
it needed a rest from trying to enlighten the zombies
hiding under rocks cushioned with dollar bills
and cocaine, their primary domain

this morning darkness reigns
what is a dream and what is real?
confusion eaten for breakfast
blind the zombies, coping by feel

this morning the sun said, enough is enough
every day I light their path get up on time,
warm their bones, inspire their rhyme
and yet they prefer the night, the dark

this morning the sun has chosen to hide
and the zombies moan loudly, harshly
spewing fiery words fiercely upon the sun's head
scaring the sun into submission

this morning the sun stood its ground
and wall street crashed instead

what I remember

what I remember is this –
the leaves whirling in the park and slapping my face
creaking with the knowledge that soon all will be gone
only bare twigs will remain, shivering in snow and icy rain
autumn has come and left me breathless
a reminder that everything in life will pass away
the warmth of summer blooms and sunny days

what I remember are the stars –
their dire warning of doom as the wind tries to blow at
the tears of children afraid to be born to this world
of hunger, scarce, disease and gloom
afraid to play and laugh, saddled with a legacy
of violence and hate, perpetuated by parents
immobilized by apathy, unable to act

what I remember are –
the teens being called upon to shoulder adult responsibility
of fixing climate change, greed, inequality and sin
unable to bear the cold wind tearing at their faces
not knowing how to piece all those leaves together again
they opt for oblivion and swallow the plentiful poisons
so easily gained in any home or street lane

what I remember about being a teen –
is having raging hormones occupying my mind
taking up all of my energy and time
without the additional burden of having to change society,
ridding it of the dirt and grime of unscrupulous hypocrisy

of false promises, lies, possessive, abusive love
Elvis on my mind, I was bereft of boxing gloves

what I know is –
and am not surprised, that suicide is on the rise
among teens that are unable to survive, they are the ones to watch
not the ones who fit in, out of touch with realty, themselves
having bought the fact that the naked emperor has clothes
the others' hopes having been dashed, hearing god is dead
and there is nothing there instead

I remember –
that a cold harsh wind is but a ray of sunshine in disguise
but who will tell the children to have this hope
alternately not telling them lies, that matter is all there is
for the young idealistic beings will have no place to hang their hats
and will find it easier to simply lie down and die or become the walking dead
I pray that parents will wake up and act before it is too late.

www.ingramcontent.com/pod-product-compliance
Lightning Source LLC
Chambersburg PA
CBHW050026170726
48282CB00025B/571
* 9 7 8 9 3 9 0 6 0 1 2 2 6 *